The Poetry Of Anne Bradstreet

Volume 1 -Quaternions

Anne Bradstreet was born in 1612 in Northampton, England. Her parents position allowed them to educate Anne across many subjects which was unusual for its day. In her teens she contracted smallpox which was to undermine her health in later years.

She married Simon at the age of sixteen. They, along with her parents, emigrated to America with other Puritans in 1630 arriving on June 14th in Massachusetts. They moved south to Charlestown almost immediately to find better conditions. After a short stay they moved yet further south to help found the 'City on the Hill' Boston. By 1632 they had moved once more, this time to Cambridge, Massachusetts where Anne gave birth to her first child, Samuel.

The family was instrumental in setting up Harvard University in 1636 but by the early 1640's pregnant with her sixth child they moved for the sixth time to Andover Parish. In all Anne bore eight children although her health was always weak.

She did however write some beautiful poetry and in 1650, the Rev. John Woodbridge had her collection of verse; The Tenth Muse Lately Sprung Up in America composed by "A Gentlewoman from Those Parts" published in London, making Anne the first female poet ever published in both England and the New World.

On July 10, 1666, their North Andover family home burned down to leave them homeless. Tragically her own personal library of some 800 books was also lost in the flames. By now, Anne's health was slowly failing. She suffered from tuberculosis and had to deal with the loss of cherished relatives. But her will remained strong and faith in God undiminished.

Anne Bradstreet died on September 16, 1672 in North Andover, Massachusetts at the age of 60.

We are pleased to present here works from her earlier years. These are quaternions, epic poems of four parts each.

Index Of Poems

Of The Four Ages Of Man
Lo, now four other act upon the stage,
Childhood and Youth, the Many and Old age:
The first son unto phlegm, grandchild to water,
Unstable, supple, cold and moist's his nature
The second, frolic, claims his pedigree
From blood and air, for hot and moist is he.
The third of fire and choler is compos'd,
Vindicative and quarrelsome dispos'd.
The last of earth and heavy melancholy,
Solid, hating all lightness and all folly.
Childhood was cloth'd in white and green to show
His spring was intermixed with some snow:
Upon his head nature a garland set
Of Primrose, Daisy and the Violet.
Such cold mean flowers the spring puts forth betime,
Before the sun hath thoroughly heat the clime.
His hobby striding did not ride but run,
And in his hand an hour-glass new begun,
In danger every moment of a fall,
And when 't is broke then ends his life and all:
But if he hold till it have run its last,
Then may he live out threescore years or past.
Next Youth came up in gorgeous attire
(As that fond age doth most of all desire),
His suit of crimson and his scarf of green,
His pride in's countenance was quickly seen;
Garland of roses, pinks and gillyflowers
Seemed on's head to grow bedew'd with showers.
His face as fresh as is Aurora fair,
When blushing she first 'gins to light the air.
No wooden horse, but one of mettle tried,
He seems to fly or swim, and not to ride.
Then prancing on the stage, about he wheels,
But as he went death waited at his heels,
The next came up in a much graver sort,
As one that cared for a good report,
His sword by's side, and choler in his eyes,
But neither us'd as yet, for he was wise;
Of Autumn's fruits a basket on his arm,
His golden god in's purse, which was his charm.
And last of all to act upon this stage
Leaning upon his staff came up Old Age,
Under his arm a sheaf of wheat he bore,

An harvest of the best, what needs he more?
In's other hand a glass ev'n almost run,
Thus writ about: "This out, then am I done."

The Four Elements

The Fire, Air, Earth and water did contest
Which was the strongest, noblest and the best,
Who was of greatest use and might'est force;
In placide Terms they thought now to discourse,
That in due order each her turn should speak;
But enmity this amity did break
All would be chief, and all scorn'd to be under
Whence issu'd winds & rains, lightning & thunder
The quaking earth did groan, the Sky lookt black
The Fire, the forced Air, in sunder crack;
The sea did threat the heav'ns, the heavn's the earth,
All looked like a Chaos or new birth:
Fire broyled Earth, & scorched Earth it choaked
Both by their darings, water so provoked
That roaring in it came, and with its source
Soon made the Combatants abate their force
The rumbling hissing, puffing was so great
The worlds confusion, it did seem to threat
Till gentle Air, Contention so abated
That betwixt hot and cold, she arbitrated
The others difference, being less did cease
All storms now laid, and they in perfect peace
That Fire should first begin, the rest consent,
The noblest and most active Element.

Of The Four Humours In Mans Constitution

The former four now ending their discourse,
Ceasing to vaunt their good, or threat their force.
Lo other four step up, crave leave to show
The native qualityes that from them flow:
But first they wisely shew'd their high descent,
Each eldest daughter to each Element.
Choler was own'd by fire, and Blood by air,
Earth knew her black swarth child, water her fair:
All having made obeysance to each Mother,
Had leave to speak, succeeding one the other:
But 'mongst themselves they were at variance,
Which of the four should have predominance.
Choler first hotly claim'd right by her mother,
Who had precedency of all the other:

But Sanguine did disdain what she requir'd,
Pleading her self was most of all desir'd.
Proud Melancholy more envious then the rest,
The second, third or last could not digest.
She was the silentest of all the four,
Her wisdom spake not much, but thought the more
Mild Flegme did not contest for chiefest place,
Only she crav'd to have a vacant space.
Well, thus they parle and chide; but to be brief,
Or will they, nill they, Choler will be chief.
They seing her impetuosity
At present yielded to necessity.
Choler.
To shew my high descent and pedegree,
Your selves would judge but vain prolixity;
It is acknowledged from whence I came,
It shall suffice to shew you what I am,
My self and mother one, as you shall see,
But shee in greater, I in less degree.
We both once Masculines, the world doth know,
Now Feminines awhile, for love we owe
Unto your Sisterhood, which makes us render
Our noble selves in a less noble gender.
Though under Fire we comprehend all heat,
Yet man for Choler is the proper seat:
I in his heart erect my regal throne,
Where Monarch like I play and sway alone.
Yet many times unto my great disgrace
One of your selves are my Compeers in place,
Where if your rule prove once predominant,
The man proves boyish, sottish, ignorant:
But if you yield subservience unto me,
I make a man, a man in th'high'st degree:
Be he a souldier, I more fence his heart
Then iron Corslet 'gainst a sword or dart.
What makes him face his foe without appal,
To storm a breach, or scale a city wall,
In dangers to account himself more sure
Then timerous Hares whom Castles do immure?
Have you not heard of worthyes, Demi-Gods?
Twixt them and others what is't makes the odds
But valour? whence comes that? from none of you,
Nay milksops at such brunts you look but blew.
Here's sister ruddy, worth the other two,
Who much will talk, but little dares she do,
Unless to Court and claw, to dice and drink,
And there she will out-bid us all, I think,

She loves a fiddle better then a drum,
A Chamber well, in field she dares not come,
She'l ride a horse as bravely as the best,
And break a staff, provided 'be in jest;
But shuns to look on wounds, & blood that's spilt,
She loves her sword only because its gilt.
Then here's our sad black Sister, worse then you.
She'l neither say she will, nor will she doe;
But peevish Malecontent, musing sits,
And by misprissions like to loose her witts:
If great perswasions cause her meet her foe,
In her dull resolution she's so slow,
To march her pace to some is greater pain
Then by a quick encounter to be slain.
But be she beaten, she'l not run away,
She'l first advise if't be not best to stay.
Now let's give cold white sister flegme her right,
So loving unto all she scorns to fight:
If any threaten her, she'l in a trice
Convert from water to congealed ice:
Her teeth will chatter, dead and wan's her face,
And 'fore she be assaulted, quits the place.
She dares not challeng, if I speak amiss,
Nor hath she wit or heat to blush at this.
Here's three of you all see now what you are,
Then yield to me preheminence in war.
Again who fits for learning, science, arts?
Who rarifies the intellectual parts:
From whence fine spirits flow and witty notions:
But tis not from our dull, slow sisters motions:
Nor sister sanguine, from thy moderate heat,
Poor spirits the Liver breeds, which is thy seat.
What comes from thence, my heat refines the same
And through the arteries sends it o're the frame:
The vital spirits they're call'd, and well they may
For when they fail, man turns unto his clay.
The animal I claim as well as these,
The nerves, should I not warm, soon would they freeze
But flegme her self is now provok'd at this
She thinks I never shot so far amiss.
The brain she challengeth, the head's her seat;
But know'ts a foolish brain that wanteth heat.
My absence proves it plain, her wit then flyes
Out at her nose, or melteth at her eyes.
Oh who would miss this influence of thine
To be distill'd, a drop on every Line?
Alas, thou hast no Spirits; thy Company

Will feed a dropsy, or a Tympany,
The Palsy, Gout, or Cramp, or some such dolour:
Thou wast not made, for Souldier or for Scholar;
Of greazy paunch, and bloated cheeks go vaunt,
But a good head from these are dissonant.
But Melancholy, wouldst have this glory thine,
Thou sayst thy wits are staid, subtil and fine;
'Tis true, when I am Midwife to thy birth
Thy self's as dull, as is thy mother Earth:
Thou canst not claim the liver, head nor heart
Yet hast the Seat assign'd, a goodly part
The sinke of all us three, the hateful Spleen
Of that black Region, nature made thee Queen;
Where pain and sore obstruction thou dost work,
Where envy, malice, thy Companions lurk.
If once thou'rt great, what follows thereupon
But bodies wasting, and destruction?
So base thou art, that baser cannot be,
Th'excrement adustion of me.
But I am weary to dilate your shame,
Nor is't my pleasure thus to blur your name,
Only to raise my honour to the Skies,
As objects best appear by contraries.
But Arms, and Arts I claim, and higher things,
The princely qualities befitting Kings,
Whose profound heads I line with policies,
They'r held for Oracles, they are so wise,
Their wrathful looks are death their words are laws
Their Courage it foe, friend, and Subject awes;
But one of you, would make a worthy King
Like our sixth Henry (that same virtuous thing)
That when a Varlet struck him o're the side,
Forsooth you are to blame, he grave reply'd.
Take Choler from a Prince, what is he more
Then a dead Lion, by Beasts triumph'd o're.
Again you know, how I act every part
By th'influence, I still send from the heart:
It's nor your Muscles, nerves, nor this nor that
Do's ought without my lively heat, that's flat:
Nay th'stomack magazine to all the rest
Without my boyling heat cannot digest:
And yet to make my greatness, still more great
What differences, the Sex? but only heat.
And one thing more, to close up my narration
Of all that lives, I cause the propagation.
I have been sparings what I might have said
I love no boasting, that's but Childrens trade.

To what you now shall say I will attend,
And to your weakness gently condescend.
Blood.
Good Sisters, give me leave, as is my place
To vent my grief, and wipe off my disgrace:
Your selves may plead your wrongs are no whit less
Your patience more then mine, I must confess
Did ever sober tongue such language speak,
Or honesty such tyes unfriendly break?
Dost know thy self so well us so amiss?
Is't arrogance or folly causeth this?
Ile only shew the wrong thou'st done to me,
Then let my sisters right their injury.
To pay with railings is not mine intent,
But to evince the truth by Argument:
I will analyse this thy proud relation
So full of boasting and prevarication,
Thy foolish incongruityes Ile show,
So walk thee till thou'rt cold, then let thee go.
There is no Souldier but thy self (thou sayest,)
No valour upon Earth, but what thou hast
Thy silly provocations I despise,
And leave't to all to judge, where valour lies
No pattern, nor no pattron will I bring
But David, Judah's most heroick King,
Whose glorious deeds in Arms the world can tell,
A rosie cheek Musitian thou know'st well;
He knew well how to handle Sword and Harp,
And how to strike full sweet, as well as sharp,
Thou laugh'st at me for loving merriment,
And scorn'st all Knightly sports at Turnament.
Thou sayst I love my Sword, because it's gilt,
But know, I love the Blade, more then the Hill,
Yet do abhor such temerarious deeds,
As thy unbridled, barbarous Choler breeds:
Thy rudeness counts good manners vanity,
And real Complements base flattery.
For drink, which of us twain like it the best,
Ile go no further then thy nose for test:
Thy other scoffs, not worthy of reply
Shall vanish as of no validity:
Of thy black Calumnies this is but part,
But now Ile shew what souldier thou art.
And though thou'st us'd me with opprobrious spight
My ingenuity must give thee right.
Thy choler is but rage when tis most pure,
But usefull when a mixture can endure;

As with thy mother fire, so tis with thee,
The best of all the four when they agree:
But let her leave the rest, then I presume
Both them and all things else she would consume.
VVhilst us for thine associates thou tak'st,
A Souldier most compleat in all points mak'st:
But when thou scorn'st to take the help we lend,
Thou art a Fury or infernal Fiend.
Witness the execrable deeds thou'st done,
Nor sparing Sex nor Age, nor Sire nor Son;
To satisfie thy pride and cruelty,
Thou oft hast broke bounds of Humanity,
Nay should I tell, thou would'st count me no blab,
How often for the lye, thou'st given the stab.
To take the wall's a sin of so high rate,
That nought but death the same may expiate,
To cross thy will, a challenge doth deserve
So shed'st that blood, thou'rt bounden to preserve
Wilt thou this valour, Courage, Manhood call:
No, know 'tis pride most diabolibal.
If murthers be thy glory, tis no less,
Ile not envy thy feats, nor happiness:
But if in fitting time and place 'gainst foes
For countreys good thy life thou dar'st expose,
Be dangers n'er so high, and courage great,
Ile praise that prowess, fury, Choler, heat:
But such thou never art when all alone,
Yet such when we all four are joyn'd in one.
And when such thou art, even such are we,
The friendly Coadjutors still of thee.
Nextly the Spirits thou dost wholly claim,
Which nat'ral, vital, animal we name:
To play Philosopher I have no list,
Nor yet Physitian, nor Anatomist,
For acting these, I have no will nor Art,
Yet shall with Equity, give thee thy part
For natural, thou dost not much contest;
For there is none (thou sayst) if some not best;
That there are some, and best, I dare averre
Of greatest use, if reason do not erre:
What is there living, which do'nt first derive
His Life now Animal, from vegetive:
If thou giv'st life, I give the nourishment,
Thine without mine, is not, 'tis evident:
But I without thy help, can give a growth
As plants trees, and small Embryon know'th
And if vital Spirits, do flow from thee

I am as sure, the natural, from me:
Be thine the nobler, which I grant, yet mine
Shall justly claim priority of thine.
I am the fountain which thy Cistern fills
Through warm blew Conduits of my venial rills:
What hath the heart, but what's sent from the liver
If thou'rt the taker, I must be the giver.
Then never boast of what thou dost receive:
For of such glory I shall thee bereave.
But why the heart should be usurp'd by thee,
I must confess seems something strange to me:
The spirits through thy heat made perfect are,
But the Materials none of thine, that's clear:
Their wondrous mixture is of blood and air,
The first my self, second my mother fair.
But Ile not force retorts, nor do thee wrong,
Thy fi'ry yellow froth is mixt among,
Challeng not all, 'cause part we do allow;
Thou know'st I've there to do as well as thou:
But thou wilt say I deal unequally,
Their lives the irascible faculty,
Which without all dispute, is Cholers own;
Besides the vehement heat, only there known
Can be imputed, unto none but Fire
Which is thy self, thy Mother and thy Sire
That this is true, I easily can assent
If still you take along my Aliment;
And let me be your partner which is due,
So shall I give the dignity to you:
Again, Stomacks Concoction thou dost claim,
But by what right, nor do'st, nor canst thou name
Unless as heat, it be thy faculty,
And so thou challengest her property.
The help she needs, the loving liver lends,
Who th'benefit o'th' whole ever intends
To meddle further I shall be but shent,
Th'rest to our Sisters is more pertinent;
Your slanders thus refuted takes no place,
Nor what you've said, doth argue my disgrace,
Now through your leaves, some little time I'l spend
My worth in humble manner to commend
This, hot, moist nutritive humour of mine
When 'tis untaint, pure, and most genuine
Shall chiefly take the place, as is my due
Without the least indignity to you.
Of all your qualities I do partake,
And what you single are, the whole I make

Your hot, moist, cold, dry natures are but four,
I moderately am all, what need I more;
As thus, if hot then dry, if moist, then cold,
If this you cann't disprove, then all I hold
My virtues hid, I've let you dimly see
My sweet Complection proves the verity.
This Scarlet die's a badge of what's within
One touch thereof, so beautifies the skin:
Nay, could I be, from all your tangs but pure
Mans life to boundless Time might still endure.
But here one thrusts her heat, wher'ts not requir'd
So suddenly, the body all is fired,
And of the calme sweet temper quite bereft,
Which makes the Mansion, by the Soul soon left.
So Melancholy seizes on a man,
With her unchearful visage, swarth and wan,
The body dryes, the mind sublime doth smother,
And turns him to the womb of's earthy mother:
And flegm likewise can shew her cruel art,
With cold distempers to pain every part:
The lungs she rots, the body wears away,
As if she'd leave no flesh to turn to clay,
Her languishing diseases, though not quick
At length demolishes the Faberick,
All to prevent, this curious care I take,
In th'last concoction segregation make
Of all the perverse humours from mine own,
The bitter choler most malignant known
I turn into his Cell close by my side
The Melancholy to the Spleen t'abide:
Likewise the whey, some use I in the veins,
The overplus I send unto the reins:
But yet for all my toil, my care and skill,
Its doom'd by an irrevocable will
That my intents should meet with interruption,
That mortal man might turn to his corruption.
I might here shew the nobleness of mind
Of such as to the sanguine are inclin'd,
They're liberal, pleasant, kind and courteous,
And like the Liver all benignious.
For arts and sciences they are the fittest;
And maugre Choler still they are the wittiest:
With an ingenious working Phantasie,
A most voluminous large Memory,
And nothing wanting but Solidity.
But why alas, thus tedious should I be,
Thousand examples you may daily see.

If time I have transgrest, and been too long,
Yet could not be more brief without much wrong;
I've scarce wip'd off the spots proud choler cast,
Such venome lies in words, though but a blast:
No braggs i've us'd, to you I dare appeal,
If modesty my worth do not conceal.
I've us'd no bittererss nor taxt your name,
As I to you, to me do ye the same.
Melancholy.
He that with two Assailants hath to do,
Had need be armed well and active too.
Especially when friendship is pretended,
That blow's most deadly where it is intended.
Though choler rage and rail, I'le not do so,
The tongue's no weapon to assault a foe:
But sith we fight with words, we might be kind
To spare our selves and beat the whistling wind,
Fair rosie sister, so might'st thou scape free;
I'le flatter for a time as thou didst me:
But when the first offender I have laid,
Thy soothing girds shall fully be repaid.
But Choler be thou cool'd or chaf'd, I'le venter,
And in contentions lists now justly enter.
What mov'd thee thus to vilifie my name,
Not past all reason, but in truth all shame:
Thy fiery spirit shall bear away this prize,
To play such furious pranks I am too wise:
If in a Souldier rashness be so precious,
Know in a General tis most pernicious.
Nature doth teach to shield the head from harm,
The blow that's aim'd thereat is latcht by th'arm.
When in Batalia my foes I face
I then command proud Choler stand thy place,
To use thy sword, thy courage and thy art
There to defend my self, thy better part.
This wariness count not for cowardize,
He is not truly valiant that's not wise.
It's no less glory to defend a town,
Then by assault to gain one not our own;
And if Marcellus bold be call'd Romes sword,
Wise Fabius is her buckler all accord:
And if thy hast my slowness should not temper,
'Twere but a mad irregular distemper;
Enough of that by our sisters heretofore,
Ile come to that which wounds me somewhat more
Of learning, policy thou wouldst bereave me,
But's not thine ignorance shall thus deceive me:

What greater Clark or Politician lives,
Then he whose brain a touch my humour gives?
What is too hot my coldness doth abate,
What's diffluent I do consolidate.
If I be partial judg'd or thought to erre,
The melancholy snake shall it aver,
Whose cold dry head more subtilty doth yield,
Then all the huge beasts of the fertile field.
Again thou dost confine me to the spleen,
As of that only part I were the Queen,
Let me as well make thy precincts the Gall,
So prison thee within that bladder small:
Reduce the man to's principles, then see
If I have not more part then all you three:
What is within, without, of theirs or thine,
Yet time and age shall soon declare it mine.
When death doth seize the man your stock is lost,
When you poor bankrupts prove then have I most.
You'l say here none shall e're disturb my right,
You high born from that lump then take your flight.
Then who's mans friend, when life & all forsakes?
His Mother mine, him to her womb retakes:
Thus he is ours, his portion is the grave,
But while he lives, I'le shew what part I have:
And first the firm dry bones I justly claim,
The strong foundation of the stately frame:
Likewise the usefull Slpeen, though not the best,
Yet is a bowel call'd well as the rest:
The Liver, Stomack, owe their thanks of right,
The first it drains, of th'last quicks appetite.
Laughter (thô thou say malice) flows from hence,
These two in one cannot have residence.
But thou most grosly dost mistake to think
The Spleen for all you three was made a sink,
Of all the rest thou'st nothing there to do,
But if thou hast, that malice is from you.
Again you often touch my swarthy hue,
That black is black, and I am black tis true;
But yet more comely far I dare avow,
Then is thy torrid nose or brazen brow.
But that which shews how high your spight is bent
Is charging me to be thy excrement:
Thy loathsome imputation I defie,
So plain a slander needeth no reply.
When by thy heat thou'st bak'd thy self to crust,
And so art call'd black Choler or adust,
Thou witless think'st that I am thy excretion,

So mean thou art in Art as in discretion:
But by your leave I'le let your greatness see
What Officer thou art to us all three,
The Kitchin Drudge, the cleanser of the sinks
That casts out all that man e're eats or drinks:
If any doubt the truth whence this should come,
Shew them thy passage to th'Duodenum;
Thy biting quality still irritates,
Till filth and thee nature exonerates:
If there thou'rt stopt, to th'Liver thou turn'st in,
And thence with jaundies saffrons all the skin.
No further time Ile spend in confutation,
I trust I've clear'd your slanderous imputation.
I now speak unto all, no more to one,
Pray hear, admire and learn instruction.
My virtues yours surpass without compare,
The first my constancy that jewel rare:
Choler's too rash this golden gift to hold,
And Sanguine is more fickle manifold,
Here, there her restless thoughts do ever fly,
Constant in nothing but unconstancy.
And what Flegme is, we know, like to her mother,
Unstable is the one, and so the other;
With me is noble patience also found,
Impatient Choler loveth not the sound,
What sanguine is, she doth not heed nor care,
Now up, now down, transported like the Air:
Flegme's patient because her nature's tame;
But I, by virtue do acquire the same.
My Temperance, Chastity is eminent,
But these with you, are seldome resident;
Now could I stain my ruddy Sisters face
With deeper red, to shew you her dsgrace,
But rather I with silence vaile her shame
Then cause her blush, while I relate the same.
Nor are ye free from this inormity,
Although she bear the greatest obloquie,
My prudence, judgement, I might now reveal
But wisdom 'tis my wisdome to conceal.
Unto diseases not inclin'd as you,
Nor cold, nor hot, Ague nor Plurisie,
Nor Cough, nor Quinsey, nor the burning Feaver,
I rarely feel to act his fierce endeavour;
My sickness in conceit chiefly doth lye,
What I imagine that's my malady.
Chymeraes strange are in my phantasy,
And things that never were, nor shall I see

I love not talk, Reason lies not in length,
Nor multitude of words argues our strength;
I've done pray sister Flegme proceed in Course,
We shall expect much sound, but little force.
Flegme.
Patient I am, patient i'd need to be,
To bear with the injurious taunts of three,
Though wit I want, and anger I have less,
Enough of both, my wrongs now to express
I've not forgot, how bitter Choler spake
Nor how her gaul on me she causeless brake;
Nor wonder 'twas for hatred there's not small,
Where opposition is Diametrical.
To what is Truth I freely will assent,
Although my Name do suffer detriment,
What's slanderous repell, doubtful dispute,
And when I've nothing left to say be mute.
Valour I want, no Souldier am 'tis true,
I'le leave that manly Property to you;
I love no thundring guns, nor bloody wars,
My polish'd Skin was not ordain'd for Skarrs:
But though the pitched field I've ever fled,
At home the Conquerours have conquered.
Nay, I could tell you what's more true then meet,
That Kings have laid their Scepters at my feet;
When Sister sanguine paints my Ivory face:
The Monarchs bend and sue, but for my grace
My lilly white when joyned with her red,
Princes hath slav'd, and Captains captived,
Country with Country, Greece with Asia fights
Sixty nine Princes, all stout Hero Knights.
Under Troys walls ten years will wear away,
Rather then loose one beauteous Helena.
But 'twere as vain, to prove this truth of mine
As at noon day, to tell the Sun doth shine.
Next difference that 'twixt us twain doth lye
Who doth possess the brain, or thou or I?
Shame forc'd the say, the matter that was mine,
But the Spirits by which it acts are thine:
Thou speakest Truth, and I can say no less,
Thy heat doth much, I candidly confess;
Yet without ostentation I may say,
I do as much for thee another way:
And though I grant, thou art my helper here,
No debtor I because it's paid else where.
With all your flourishes, now Sisters three
Who is't that dare, or can, compare with me,

My excellencies are so great, so many,
I am confounded; fore I speak of any:
The brain's the noblest member all allow,
Its form and Scituation will avow,
Its Ventricles, Membranes and wondrous net,
Galen, Hippocrates drive to a set;
That Divine Ofspring the immortal Soul
Though it in all, and every part be whole,
Within this stately place of eminence,
Doth doubtless keep its mighty residence.
And surely, the Soul sensitive here lives,
Which life and motion to each creature gives,
The Conjugation of the parts, to th'braine
Doth shew, hence flow the pow'rs which they retain
Within this high Built Cittadel, doth lye
The Reason, fancy, and the memory;
The faculty of speech doth here abide,
The Spirits animal, from hence do slide:
The five most noble Senses here do dwell;
Of three it's hard to say, which doth excell.
This point now to discuss, 'longs not to me,
I'le touch the sight, great'st wonder of the three;
The optick Nerve, Coats, humours all are mine,
The watry, glassie, and the Chrystaline;
O mixture strange! O colour colourless,
Thy perfect temperament who can express:
He was no fool who thought the soul lay there,
Whence her affections passions speak so clear.
O good, O bad, O true, O traiterous eyes
What wonderments within your Balls there lyes,
Of all the Senses sight shall be the Queen;
Yet some may wish, O had mine eyes ne're seen.
Mine, likewise is the marrow, of the back,
Which runs through all the Spondles of the rack,
It is the substitute o'th royal brain,
All Nerves, except seven pair, to it retain.
And the strong Ligaments from hence arise,
Which joynt to joynt, the intire body tyes.
Some other parts there issue from the Brain,
Whose worth and use to tell, I must refrain:
Some curious learned Crooke, may these reveal
But modesty, hath charg'd me to conceal
Here's my Epitome of excellence:
For what's the Brains is mine by Consequence.
A foolish brain (quoth Choler) wanting heat
But a mad one say I, where 'tis too great,
Phrensie's worse then folly, one would more glad

With a tame fool converse then with a mad;
For learning then my brain is not the fittest,
Nor will I yield that Choler is the wittiest.
Thy judgement is unsafe, thy fancy little,
For memory the sand is not more brittle;
Again, none's fit for Kingly state but thou,
If Tyrants be the best, I le it allow:
But if love be as requisite as fear,
Then thou and I must make a mixture here.
Well to be brief, I hope now Cholers laid,
And I'le pass by what Sister sanguine said.
To Melancholy I le make no reply,
The worst she said was instability,
And too much talk, both which I here confess
A warning good, hereafter I'le say less.
Let's now be friends; its time our spight were spent,
Lest we too late this rashness do repent,
Such premises will force a sad conclusion,
Unless we agree, all falls into confusion.
Let Sangine with her hot hand Choler hold,
To take her moist my moisture will be bold:
My cold, cold melancholy hand shall clasp;
Her dry, dry Cholers other hand shall grasp.
Two hot, two moist, two cold, two dry here be,
A golden Ring, the Posey VNITY.
Nor jarrs nor scoffs, let none hereafter see,
But all admire our perfect Amity
Nor be discern'd, here's water, earth, air, fire,
But here a compact body, whole intire.
This loving counsel pleas'd them all so well
That flegm was judg'd for kindness to excell.

The Four Seasons
Spring.
Another four I've left yet to bring on,
Of four times four the last Quaternion,
The Winter, Summer, Autumn & the Spring,
In season all these Seasons I shall bring:
Sweet Spring like man in his Minority,
At present claim'd, and had priority.
With smiling face and garments somewhat green,
She trim'd her locks, which late had frosted been,
Nor hot nor cold, she spake, but with a breath,
Fit to revive, the nummed earth from death.
Three months (quoth she) are 'lotted to my share

March, April, May of all the rest most fair.
Tenth of the first, Sol into Aries enters,
And bids defiance to all tedious winters,
Crosseth the Line, and equals night and day,
(Stil adds to th'last til after pleasant May)
And now makes glad the darkned northern wights
Who for some months have seen but starry lights.
Now goes the Plow-man to his merry toyle,
He might unloose his winter locked soyl:
The Seeds-man too, doth lavish out his grain,
In hope the more he casts, the more to gain:
The Gardner now superfluous branches lops,
And poles erects for his young clambring hops.
Now digs then sowes his herbs, his flowers & roots
And carefully manures his trees of fruits.
The Pleiades their influence now give,
And all that seem'd as dead afresh doth live.
The croaking frogs, whom nipping winter kil'd
Like birds now chirp, and hop about the field,
The Nightingale, the black-bird and the Thrush
Now tune their layes, on sprayes of every bush.
The wanton frisking Kid, and soft-fleec'd Lambs
Do jump and play before their feeding Dams,
The tender tops of budding grass they crop,
They joy in what they have, but more in hope:
For though the frost hath lost his binding power,
Yet many a fleece of snow and stormy shower
Doth darken Sol's bright eye, makes us remember
The pinching North-west wind of cold December.
My second moneth is April, green and fair,
Of longer dayes, and a more temperate Air:
The Sun in Taurus keeps his residence,
And with his warmer beams glanceth from thence
This is the month whose fruitful showrs produces
All set and sown for all delights and uses:
The Pear, the Plum, and Apple-tree now flourish
The grass grows long the hungry beast to nourish.
The Primrose pale, and azure violet
Among the virduous grass hath nature set,
That when the Sun on's Love (the earth) doth shine
These might as lace set out her garment fine.
The fearfull bird his little house now builds
In trees and walls, in Cities and in fields.
The outside strong, the inside warm and neat;
A natural Artificer compleat.
The clocking hen her chirping chickins leads
With wings & beak defends them from the gleads

My next and last is fruitfull pleasant May,
Wherein the earth is clad in rich aray,
The Sun now enters loving Gemini,
And heats us with the glances of his eye,
Our thicker rayment makes us lay aside
Lest by his fervor we be torrifi'd.
All flowers the Sun now with his beams discloses,
Except the double pinks and matchless Roses.
Now swarms the busy, witty, honey-Bee,
VVhose praise deserves a page from more then me
The cleanly Huswifes Dary's now in th'prime,
Her shelves and firkins fill'd for winter time.
The meads with Cowslips, Honey-suckles dight,
One hangs his head, the other stands upright:
But both rejoyce at th'heavens clear smiling face,
More at her showers, which water them a space.
For fruits my Season yields the early Cherry,
The hasty Peas, and wholsome cool Strawberry.
More solid fruits require a longer time,
Each Season hath his fruit, so hath each Clime:
Each man his own peculiar excellence,
But none in all that hath preheminence.
Sweet fragrant Spring, with thy short pittance fly
Let some describe thee better then can I.
Yet above all this priviledg is thine,
Thy dayes still lengthen without least decline:
Summer.
When Spring had done, the Summer did begin,
With melted tauny face, and garments thin,
Resembling Fire, Choler, and Middle age,
As Spring did Air, Blood, Youth in's equipage.
Wiping the sweat from of her face that ran,
With hair all wet she puffing thus began;
Bright June, July and August hot are mine,
In'th first Sol doth in crabbed Cancer shine.
His progress to the North now's fully done,
Then retrograde must be my burning Sun,
Who to his southward Tropick still is bent,
Yet doth his parching heat but more augment
Though he decline, because his flames so fair,
Have throughly dry'd the earth, and heat the air.
Like as an Oven that long time hath been heat,
Whose vehemency at length doth grow so great,
That if you do withdraw her burning store,
Tis for a time as fervent as before.
Now go those frolick Swains, the Shepherd Lads
To wash the thick cloth'd flocks with pipes full glad

In the cool streams they labour with delight
Rubbing their dirty coats till they look white:
Whose fleece when finely spun and deeply dy'd
With Robes thereof Kings have been dignifi'd.
Blest rustick Swains, your pleasant quiet life,
Hath envy bred in Kings that were at strife,
Careless of worldly wealth you sing and pipe,
Whilst they'r imbroyl'd in wars & troubles rise:
VVhich made great Bajazet cry out in's woes,
Oh happy shepherd which hath not to lose.
Orthobulus, nor yet Sebastia great,
But whist'leth to thy flock in cold and heat.
Viewing the Sun by day, the Moon by night
Endimions, Dianaes dear delight,
Upon the grass resting your healthy limbs,
By purling Brooks looking how fishes swims.
If pride within your lowly Cells ere haunt,
Of him that was Shepherd then King go vaunt.
This moneth the Roses are distil'd in glasses,
VVhose fragrant smel all made perfumes surpasses
The Cherry, Gooseberry are now in th'prime,
And for all sorts of Pease, this is the time.
July my next, the hott'st in all the year,
The sun through Leo now takes his Career,
VVhose flaming breath doth melt us from afar,
Increased by the star Canicular.
This Month from Julius Cæsar took its name,
By Romans celebrated to his fame.
Now go the Mowers to their slashing toyle,
The Meadowes of their riches to dispoyle,
VVith weary strokes, they take all in their way,
Bearing the burning heat of the long day.
The forks and Rakes do follow them amain,
VVhich makes the aged fields look young again.
The groaning Carts do bear away this prize.
To Stacks and Barns where it for Fodder lyes.
My next and last is August fiery hot
(For much, the Southward Sun abateth not)
This Moneth he keeps with Virgo for a space,
The dryed Earth is parched with his face.
August of great Augustus took its name,
Romes second Emperour of lasting fame,
With sickles now the bending Reapers goe
The russling tress of terra down to mowe;
And bundles up in sheaves, the weighty wheat,
Which after Manchet makes for Kings to eat:
The Barly, Rye and Pease should first had place,

Although their bread have not so white a face.
The Carter leads all home with whistling voyce,
He plow'd with pain, but reaping doth rejoyce;
His sweat, his toyle, his careful wakeful nights,
His fruitful Crop abundantly requites.
Now's ripe the Pear, Pear-plumb, and Apricock,
The prince of plumbs, whose stone's as hard as Rock
The Summer seems but short, the Autumn hasts
To shake his fruits, of most delicious tasts
Like good old Age, whose younger juicy Roots
Hath still ascended, to bear goodly fruits.
Until his head be gray, and strength be gone.
Yet then appears the worthy deeds he'th done:
To feed his boughs exhausted hath his sap,
Then drops his fruits into the eaters lap.
Autumn.
Of Autumn moneths September is the prime,
Now day and night are equal in each Clime,
The twelfth of this Sol riseth in the Line,
And doth in poizing Libra this month shine.
The vintage now is ripe, the grapes are prest,
Whose lively liquor oft is curs'd and blest:
For nought so good, but it may be abused,
But its a precious juice when well its used.
The raisins now in clusters dryed be,
The Orange, Lemon dangle on the tree:
The Pomegranate, the Fig are ripe also,
And Apples now their yellow sides do show.
Of Almonds, Quinces, Wardens, and of Peach,
The season's now at hand of all and each.
Sure at this time, time first of all began,
And in this moneth was made apostate Man:
For then in Eden was not only seen,
Boughs full of leaves, or fruits unripe or green,
Or withered stocks, which were all dry and dead,
But trees with goodly fruits replenished;
Which shews nor Summer, Winter nor the Spring
Our Grand-Sire was of Paradice made King:
Nor could that temp'rate Clime such difference make,
If scited as the most Judicious take.
October is my next, we hear in this
The Northern winter-blasts begin to hiss.
In Scorpio resideth now the Sun,
And his declining heat is almost done.
The fruitless Trees all withered now do stand,
Whose sapless yellow leavs, by winds are fan'd,
Which notes when youth and strength have past their prime

Decrepit age must also have its time.
The Sap doth slily creep towards the Earth
There rests, until the Sun give it a birth.
So doth old Age still tend unto his grave,
Where also he his winter time must have;
But when the Sun of righteousness draws nigh,
His dead old stock, shall mount again on high.
November is my last, for Time doth haste,
We now of winters sharpness 'gins to tast.
This moneth the Sun's in Sagitarius,
So farre remote, his glances warm not us.
Almost at shortest is the shorten'd day,
The Northern pole beholdeth not one ray.
Now Greenland, Groanland, Finland, Lapland, see
No Sun, to lighten their obscurity:
Poor wretches that in total darkness lye,
With minds more dark then is the dark'ned Sky.
Beaf, Brawn, and Pork are now in great request,
And solid meats our stomacks can digest.
This time warm cloaths, full diet, and good fires,
Our pinched flesh, and hungry mawes requires:
Old, cold, dry Age and Earth Autumn resembles,
And Melancholy which most of all dissembles.
I must be short, and shorts, the short'ned day,
What winter hath to tell, now let him say.
Winter.
Cold, moist, young flegmy winter now doth lye
In swadling Clouts, like new born Infancy
Bound up with frosts, and furr'd with hail & snows,
And like an Infant, still it taller grows;
December is my first, and now the Sun
To th'Southward Tropick, his swift race doth run:
This moneth he's hous'd in horned Capricorn,
From thence he 'gins to length the shortned morn,
Through Christendome with great Feastivity,
Now's held, (but ghest) for blest Nativity.
Cold frozen January next comes in,
Chilling the blood and shrinking up the skin;
In Aquarius now keeps the long wisht Sun,
And Northward his unwearied Course doth run:
The day much longer then it was before,
The cold not lessened, but augmented more.
Now Toes and Ears, and Fingers often freeze,
And Travellers their noses sometimes leese.
Moist snowie February is my last,
I care not how the winter time doth haste.
In Pisces now the golden Sun doth shine,

And Northward still approaches to the Line,
The Rivers 'gin to ope, the snows to melt,
And some warm glances from his face are felt;
Which is increased by the lengthen'd day,
Until by's heat, he drive all cold away,
And thus the year in Circle runneth round:
Where first it did begin, in th'end its found.
My Subjects bare, my Brain is bad,
Or better Lines you should have had:
The first fell in so nat'rally,
I knew not how to pass it by;
The last, though bad I could not mend,
Accept therefore of what is pen'd,
And all the faults that you shall spy
Shall at your feet for pardon cry.

The Four Monarchyes, The Assyrian Being The First, Beginning Under Nimrod, 131 Years After The Flood

When time was young, & World in Infancy,
Man did not proudly strive for Soveraignty:
But each one thought his petty Rule was high,
If of his house he held the Monarchy.
This was the golden Age, but after came
The boisterous son of Chus, Grand-Child to Ham,
That mighty Hunter, who in his strong toyles
Both Beasts and Men subjected to his spoyles:
The strong foundation of proud Babel laid,
Erech, Accad, and Culneh also made.
These were his first, all stood in Shinar land,
From thence he went Assyria to command,
And mighty Niniveh, he there begun,
Not finished till he his race had run.
Resen, Caleh, and Rehoboth likewise
By him to Cities eminent did rise.
Of Saturn, he was the Original,
Whom the succeeding times a God did call,
When thus with rule, he had been dignifi'd,
One hundred fourteen years he after dy'd.
Belus.
Great Nimrod dead, Belus the next his Son
Confirms the rule, his Father had begun;
Whose acts and power is not for certainty
Left to the world, by any History.
But yet this blot for ever on him lies,
He taught the people first to Idolize:
Titles Divine he to himself did take,

Alive and dead, a God they did him make.
This is that Bel the Chaldees worshiped,
Whose Priests in Stories oft are mentioned;
This is that Baal to whom the Israelites
So oft profanely offered sacred Rites:
This is Beelzebub God of Ekronites,
Likewise Baalpeor of the Mohabites,
His reign was short, for as I calculate,
At twenty five ended his Regal date.
Ninus.
His Father dead, Ninus begins his reign,
Transfers his seat to the Assyrian plain;
And mighty Nineveh more mighty made,
Whose Foundation was by his Grand-sire laid:
Four hundred forty Furlongs wall'd about,
On which stood fifteen hundred Towers stout.
The walls one hundred sixty foot upright,
So broad three Chariots run abrest there might.
Upon the pleasant banks of Tygris floud
This stately Seat of warlike Ninus stood:
This Ninus for a God his Father canonized,
To whom the sottish people sacrificed.
This Tyrant did his Neighbours all oppress,
Where e're he warr'd he had too good success.
Barzanes the great Armenian King
By force and fraud did under Tribute bring.
The Median Country he did also gain,
Thermus their King he caused to be slain;
An Army of three millions he led out
Against the Bactrians (but that I doubt)
Zoreaster their King he likewise slew,
And all the greater Asia did subdue.
Semiramis from Menon did he take
Then drown'd himself, did Menon for her sake.
Fifty two years he reign'd, (as we are told)
The world then was two thousand nineteen old.
Semiramis.
This great oppressing Ninus, dead and gone,
His wife Semiramis usurp'd the Throne;
She like a brave Virago played the Rex
And was both shame and glory of her Sex:
Her birth place was Philistines Ascolan,
Her mother Dorceta a Curtizan.
Others report she was a vestal Nun,
Adjudged to be drown'd for th'crime she'd done.
Transform'd into a Fish by Venus will,
Her beauteous face, (they feign) reteining still.

Sure from this Fiction Dagon first began,
Changing the womans face into a man:
But all agree that from no lawfull bed,
This great renowned Empress issued:
For which she was obscurely nourished,
Whence rose that Fable, she by birds was fed.
This gallant Dame unto the Bactrian warre,
Accompanying her husband Menon farr,
Taking a town, such valour she did show,
That Ninus amorous of her soon did grow,
And thought her fit to make a Monarchs wife,
Which was the cause poor Menon lost his life:
She flourishing with Ninus long did reign,
Till her Ambition caus'd him to be slain.
That having no Compeer, she might rule all,
Or else she sought revenge for Menon's fall.
Some think the Greeks this slander on her cast,
As on her life Licentious, and unchast,
That undeserv'd, they blur'd her name and fame
By their aspersions, cast upon the same:
But were her virtues more or less, or none,
She for her potency must go alone.
Her wealth she shew'd in building Babylon,
Admir'd of all, but equaliz'd of none;
The Walls so strong, and curiously was wrought,
That after Ages, Skill by them was taught:
With Towers and Bulwarks made of costly stone,
Quadrangle was the form it stood upon.
Each Square was fifteen thousand paces long,
An hundred gates it had of mettal strong:
Three hundred sixty foot the walls in height,
Almost incredible, they were in breadth
Some writers say, six Chariots might affront
With great facility, march safe upon't:
About the Wall a ditch so deep and wide,
That like a River long it did abide.
Three hundred thousand men here day by day
Bestow'd their labour, and receiv'd their pay.
And that which did all cost and Art excell,
The wondrous Temple was, she rear'd to Bell:
Which in the midst of this brave Town was plac'd,
Continuing till Xerxes it defac'd:
Whose stately top above the Clouds did rise,
From whence Astrologers oft view'd the Skies.
This to describe in each particular,
A structure rare I should but rudely marre.
Her Gardens, Bridges, Arches, mounts and spires

All eyes that saw, or Ears that hear admires,
In Shinar plain on the Euphratian flood
This wonder of the world, this Babel stood.
An expedition to the East she made
Staurobates, his Country to invade:
Her Army of four millions did consist,
Each may believe it as his fancy list.
Her Camels, Chariots, Gallyes in such number,
As puzzles best Historians to remember;
But this is wonderful, of all those men,
They say, but twenty e're came back agen.
The River Judas swept them half away,
The rest Staurobates in fight did slay;
This was last progress of this mighty Queen,
Who in her Country never more was seen.
The Poets feign'd her turn'd into a Dove,
Leaving the world to Venus soar'd above:
Which made the Assyrians many a day,
A Dove within their Ensigns to display:
Forty two years she reign'd, and then she di'd
But by what means we are not certifi'd.
Ninias or Zamies.
His Mother dead, Ninias obtains his right,
A Prince wedded to ease and to delight,
Or else was his obedience very great,
To sit thus long (obscure) rob'd of his Seat.
Some write his Mother put his habit on,
Which made the people think they serv'd her Son:
But much it is, in more then forty years
This fraud in war nor peace at all appears:
More like it is his lust with pleasures fed,
He sought no rule till she was gone and dead.
VVhat then he did of worth can no man tell,
But is suppos'd to be that Amraphel
VVho warr'd with Sodoms and Gomorrahs King,
'Gainst whom his trained bands Abram did bring,
But this is farre unlike, he being Son
Unto a Father, that all Countryes won
So suddenly should loose so great a state,
VVith petty Kings to joyne Confederate.
Nor can those Reasons which wise Raileih finds,
VVell satisfie the most considerate minds:
VVe may with learned Vsher better say,
He many Ages liv'd after that day.
And that Semiramis then flourished
VVhen famous Troy was so beleaguered:
VVhat e're he was, or did, or how it fell,

VVe may suggest our thoughts but cannot tell.
For Ninias and all his race are left
In deep oblivion, of acts bereft:
And many hundred years in silence sit,
Save a few Names a new Berosus writ.
And such as care not what befalls their fames,
May feign as many acts as he did Names;
It may suffice, if all be true that's past.
T'Sardanapalas next, we will make haste.
Sardanapalas
Sardanapalas, Son to Ocrazapes,
VVho wallowed in all voluptuousness,
That palliardizing sot that out of dores,
Ne're shew'd his face but revell'd with his whores
Did wear their garbs, their gestures imitate,
And in their kind, t'excel did emulate.
His baseness knowing, and the peoples hate
Kept close, fearing his well deserved fate;
It chanc'd Arbaces brave unwarily,
His Master like a Strumpet clad did spye.
His manly heart disdained (in the least)
Longer to serve this Metamorphos'd Beast;
Unto Belosus then he brake his mind,
Who sick of his disease, he soon did find
These two, rul'd Media and Babilon
Both for their King, held their Dominion;
Belosus promised Arbaces aid,
Arbaces him fully to be repayd.
The last: The Medes and Persians do invite
Against their monstrous King, to use their might.
Belosus, the Chaldeans doth require
And the Arabians, to further his desire:
These all agree, and forty thousand make
The Rule, from their unworthy Prince to take:
These Forces mustered. and in array
Sardanapalus leaves his Apish play.
And though of wars, he did abhor the sight;
Fear of his diadem did force him fight:
And either by his valour, or his fate,
Arbaces Courage he did so abate;
That in dispair, he left the Field and fled,
But with fresh hopes Belosus succoured,
From Bactria, an Army was at hand
Prest for this Service by the Kings Command:
These with celerity Arbaces meet,
And with all Terms of amity them greet.
With promises their necks now to unyoke,

And their Taxations sore all to revoke;
T'infranchise them, to grant what they could crave,
No priviledge to want, Subjects should have,
Only intreats them, to joyn their Force with his,
And win the Crown, which was the way to bliss.
Won by his loving looks, more by his speech,
T'accept of what they could, they all beseech:
Both sides their hearts their hands, & bands unite,
And set upon their Princes Camp that night;
Who revelling in Cups, sung care away,
For victory obtain'd the other day:
And now surpris'd, by this unlookt for fright,
Bereft of wits, were slaughtered down right.
The King his brother leavs, all to sustain,
And speeds himself to Niniveh amain.
But Salmeneus slain, the Army falls;
The King's pursu'd unto the City Walls,
But he once in, pursuers came to late,
The Walls and Gates their hast did terminate,
There with all store he was so well provided:
That what Arbaces did, was but derided:
Who there incamp'd, two years for little end,
But in the third, the River prov'd his friend,
For by the rain, was Tygris so o'reflown,
Part of that stately Wall was overthrown.
Arbaces marches in the Town he takes,
For few or none (it seems) resistance makes:
And now they saw fulfil'd a Prophesy,
That when the River prov'd their Enemy,
Their strong wal'd Town should suddenly be taken
By this accomplishment, their hearts were shaken.
Sardanapalas did not seek to fly,
This his inevitable destiny;
But all his wealth and friends together gets,
Then on himself, and them a fire he sets.
This was last Monarch of great Ninus race
That for twelve hundred years had held the place;
Twenty he reign'd same time, as Stories tell,
That Amaziah was King of Israel.
His Father was then King (as we suppose)
VVhen Jonah for their sins denounc'd those woes.
He did repent, the threatning was not done,
But now accomplish'd in his wicked Son.
Arbaces thus of all becoming Lord,
Ingeniously with all did keep his word.
Of Babylon Belosus he made King,
VVith overplus of all the wealth therein.

To Bactrians he gave their liberty,
Of Ninivites he caused none to dye.
But suffer'd with their goods, to go else where,
Not granting them now to inhabit there:
For he demolished that City great,
And unto Media transfer'd his Seat.
Such was his promise which he firmly made,
To Medes and Persians when he crav'd their aid:
A while he and his race aside must stand,
Not pertinent to what we have in hand;
And Belochus in's progeny pursue,
VVho did this Monarchy begin anew.
Belosus or Belochus.
Belosus setled in his new old Seat,
Not so content but aiming to be great,
Incroaching still upon the bordering lands,
Till Mesopotamia he got in's hands.
And either by compound or else by strength,
Assyria he gain'd also at length;
Then did rebuild, destroyed Nineveh,
A costly work which none could do but he,
VVho own'd the Treasures of proud Babylon,
And those that seem'd with Snrdanapal's gone;
For though his Palace did in ashes lye,
The fire those Mettals could not damnifie;
From these with diligence he rakes,
Arbaces suffers all, and all he takes,
He thus inricht by this new tryed gold.
Raises a Phænix new, from grave o'th' old;
And from this heap did after Ages see
As fair a Town, as the first Niniveh.
VVhen this was built, and matters all in peace
Molests poor Israel, his wealth t'increase.
A thousand Talents of Menahem had,
(Who to be rid of such a guest was glad
In sacrid writ he's known by name of Pul,
Which makes the world of difference so full.
That he and Belochus could not one be,
But Circumstance doth prove the verity;
And times of both computed so fall out,
That these two made but one, we need not doubt:
What else he did, his Empire to advance,
To rest content we must, in ignorance.
Forty eight years he reign'd, his race then run,
He left his new got Kingdome to his Son.
Tiglath Pulassar.
Belosus dead, Tiglath his warlike Son,

Next treads those steps, by which his Father won;
Damascus ancient Seat, of famous Kings
Under subjection, by his Sword he brings.
Resin their valiant King he also slew,
And Syria t'obedience did subdue.
Judas bad King occasioned this war,
When Resins force his Borders sore did marre,
And divers Cities by strong hand did seaze:
To Tiglath then, doth Ahaz send for ease,
The Temple robs, so to fulfil his ends,
And to Assyria's King a present sends.
I am thy Servant and thy Son, (quoth he)
From Resin, and from Pekah set me free,
Gladly doth Tiglath this advantage take,
And succours Ahaz, yet for Tiglath's sake.
Then Resin slain, his Army overthrown,
He Syria makes a Province of his own.
Unto Damascus then comes Judah's King,
His humble thankfulness (in haste) to bring,
Acknowledging th'Assyrians high desert,
To whom he ought all loyalty of heart.
But Tiglath having gain'd his wished end,
Proves unto Ahaz but a feigned friend;
All Israels lands beyond Jordan he takes,
In Galilee he woful havock makes.
Through Syria now he march'd none stopt his way,
And Ahaz open at his mercy lay;
Who still implor'd his love, but was distrest;
This was that Ahaz, who so high trans grest:
Thus Tiglath reign'd, & warr'd twenty seven years
Then by his death releas'd was Israels fears.
Salmanassar or Nabanassar.
Tiglath deceas'd, Salmanassar was next,
He Israelites, more then his Father vext;
Hoshea their last King he did invade,
And him six years his Tributary made;
But weary of his servitude, he sought
To Egypts King, which did avail him nought;
For Salmanassar with a mighty Host,
Besieg'd his Regal Town, and spoyl'd his Coast,
And did the people, nobles, and their King,
Into perpetual thraldome that time bring;
Those that from Joshuah's time had been a state,
Did Justice now by him eradicate:
This was that strange, degenerated brood,
On whom, nor threats, nor mercies could do good;
Laden with honour, prisoners, and with spoyle,

Returns triumphant Victor to his soyle;
He placed Israel there, where he thought best,
Then sent his Colonies, theirs to invest;
Thus Jacobs Sons in Exile must remain,
And pleasant Canaan never saw agaiu:
Where now those ten Tribes are, can no man tell,
Or how they fare, rich, poor, or ill, or well;
Whether the Indians of the East, or West,
Or wild Tartarians, as yet ne're blest,
Or else those Chinoes rare, whose wealth & arts
Hath bred more wonder then belief in hearts:
But what, or where they are; yet know we this,
They shall return, and Zion see with bliss.
Senacherib.
Senacherib Salmanasser succeeds,
Whose haughty heart is showne in words & deeds
His wars, none better then himself can boast,
On Henah, Arpad, and on Juahs coast;
On Hevahs and on Shepharvaims gods,
'Twixt them and Israels he knew no odds,
Untill the thundring hand of heaven he felt,
Which made his Army into nothing melt:
With shame then turn'd to Ninive again,
And by his sons in's Idols house was slain.
Essarhadon.
His Son, weak Essarhaddon reign'd in's place,
The fifth, and last of great Bellosus race.
Brave Merodach, the Son of Baladan,
In Babylon Lieftenant to this man
Of opportunity advantage takes,
And on his Masters ruines his house makes,
As Belosus his Soveraign did onthrone,
So he's now stil'd the King of Babilon.
After twelve years did Essarhaddon dye,
And Merodach assume the Monarchy.
Merodach Balladan.
All yield to him, but Niniveh kept free,
Untill his Grand-child made her bow the knee.
Ambassadors to Hezekiah sent,
His health congratulates with complement.
Ben Merodach.
Ben MERODACH Successor to this King,
Of whom is little said in any thing,
But by conjecture this, and none but he
Led King Manasseh to Captivity.
Nebulassar.
Brave Nebulassar to this King was son,

The famous Niniveh by him was won,
For fifty years, or more, it had been free,
Now yields her neck unto captivity:
A Vice-Roy from her foe she's glad to accept,
By whom in firm obedience she is kept.
This King's less fam'd for all the acts he's done,
Then being Father to so great a Son.
Nebuchadnezzar, or Nebopolassar.
The famous acts of this heroick King
Did neither Homer, Hesiod, Virgil sing:
Nor of his Wars have we the certainty
From some Thucidides grave history;
Nor's Metamorphosis from Ovids book,
Nor his restoriag from old Legends took:
But by the Prophets, Pen-men most divine,
This prince in's magnitude doth ever shine:
This was of Monarchyes that head of gold,
The richest and the dread fullest to behold:
This was that tree whose branches fill'd the earth,
Under whose shadow birds and beasts had birth:
This was that king of kings, did what he pleas'd,
Kil'd, sav'd, pul'd down, set up, or pain'd or eas'd;
And this was he, who when he fear'd the least
Was changed from a King into a beast.
This Prince the last year of his fathers reign
Against Jehojakim marcht with his train,
Judahs poor King besieg'd and succourless
Yields to his mercy, and the present 'stress;
His Vassal is, gives pledges for his truth,
Children of royal blood, unblemish'd youth:
Wise Daniel and his fellowes, mongst the rest,
By the victorious king to Babel's prest:
The Temple of rich ornaments defac'd,
And in his Idols house the vessels plac'd.
The next year he with unresisted hand
Quite vanguish'd Pharaoh Necho with his band:
By great Euphrates did his army fall,
Which was the loss of Syria withall.
Then into Egypt Necho did retire,
Which in few years proves the Assirians hire.
A mighty army next he doth prepare,
And unto wealthy Tyre in hast repair.
Such was the scituation of this place,
As might not him, but all the world out-face,
That in her pride she knew not which to boast
Whether her wealth, or yet her strength was most
How in all merchandize she did excel,

None but the true Ezekiel need to tell.
And for her strength, how hard she was to gain,
Can Babels tired souldiers tell with pain.
Within an Island had this city seat,
Divided from the Main by channel great:
Of costly ships and Gallyes she had store,
And Mariners to handle sail and oar:
But the Chaldeans had nor ships nor skill,
Their shoulders must their Masters mind fulfill,
Fetcht rubbish from the opposite old town,
And in the channel threw each burden down;
Where after many essayes, they made at last
The sea firm land, whereon the Army past,
And took the wealthy town; but all the gain,
Requited not the loss, the toyle and pain.
Full thirteen years in this strange work he spent
Before he could accomplish his intent:
And though a Victor home his Army leads,
With peeled shoulders, and with balded heads.
When in the Tyrian war this King was hot,
Jehojakim his oath had clean forgot,
Thinks this the fittest time to break his bands
Whilest Babels King thus deep engaged stands:
But he whose fortunes all were in the ebbe,
Had all his hopes like to a spiders web;
For this great King withdraws part of his force,
To Judah marches with a speedy course,
And unexpected finds the feeble Prince
Whom he chastis'd thus for his proud offence,
Fast bound, intends to Babel him to send,
But chang'd his mind, & caus'd his life there end,
Then cast him out like to a naked Ass,
For this is he for whom none said alas.
His son he suffered three months to reign,
Then from his throne he pluck'd him down again,
Whom with his mother he to Babel led,
And seven and thirty years in prison fed:
His Uncle he establish'd in his place
(Who was last King of holy Davids race)
But he as perjur'd as Jehojakim,
They lost more now then e're they lost by him.
Seven years he kept his faith, and safe he dwells;
But in the eighth against his Prince rebels:
The ninth came Nebuchadnezzar with power,
Besieg'd his city, temple, Zions tower,
And after eighteen months he took them all:
The Walls so strong, that stood so long, now fall.

The cursed King by flight could no wise fly
His well deserv'd and foretold misery:
But being caught to Babels wrathfull King
With children, wives and Nobles all they bring,
Where to the sword all but himself were put,
And with that wofull sight his eyes close shut.
Ah! hapless man, whose darksome contemplation
Was nothing but such gastly meditation.
In midst of Babel now till death he lyes;
Yet as was told ne're saw it with his eyes.
The Temple's burnt, the vessels had away.
The towres and palaces brought to decay:
Where late of harp and Lute were heard the noise
Now Zim & Jim lift up their scrieching voice.
All now of worth are Captive led with tears,
And sit bewailing Zion seventy years.
With all these conquests, Babels King rests not,
No not when Moab, Edom he had got,
Kedar and Hazar, the Arabians too,
All Vassals at his hands for Grace must sue.
A total conquest of rich Egypt makes,
All rule he from the ancient Phraohes takes,
Who had for sixteen hundred years born sway,
To Babilons proud King now yields the day.
Then Put and Lud do at his mercy stand.
VVhere e're he goes, he conquers every land.
His sumptuous buildings passes all conceit,
Which wealth and strong ambition made so great.
His Image Judahs Captives worship not,
Although the Furnace be seven times more hot.
His dreams wise Daniel doth expound full well,
And his unhappy chang with grief foretell.
Strange melancholy humours on him lay,
Which for seven years his reason took away,
VVhich from no natural causes did proceed,
But for his pride, so had the heavens decreed.
The time expir'd, bruitish remains no more,
But Government resumes as heretofore:
In splendor, and in Majesty he sits,
Contemplating those times he lost his witts.
And if by words we may ghess at the heart,
This king among the righteous had a part:
Fourty four years he reign'd, which being run,
He left his wealth and conquests to his son.
Evilmerodach
Babel's great Monarch now laid in the dust,
His son possesses wealth and rule as just:

And in the first year of his Royalty
Easeth Jehojakims Captivity:
Poor forlorn Prince, who had all state forgot
In seven and thirty years had seen no jot.
Among the conquer'd Kings that there did ly
Is Judah's King now lifted up on high:
But yet in Babel he must still remain,
And native Canaan never see again:
Unlike his Father Evilmerodach,
Prudence and·magnanimity did lack;
Fair Egypt is by his remisness lost,
Arabia, and all the bordering coast.
Warrs with the Medes unhappily he wag'd
(Within which broyles rich Croesus was ingag'd)
His Army routed, and himself there slain:
His Kingdome to Belshazzar did remain.
Belshazzar.
Unworthy Belshazzar next wears the crown,
Whose acts profane a sacred Pen sets down,
His lust and crueltyes in storyes find,
A royal State rul'd by a bruitish mind.
His life so base, and dissolute invites
The noble Persian to invade his rights.
Who with his own, and Uncles power anon,
Layes siedge to's Regal Seat, proud Babylon,
The coward King, whose strength lay in his walls,
To banquetting and revelling now falls,
To shew his little dread, but greater store,
To chear his friends, and scorn his foes the more.
The holy vessels thither brought long since,
They carrows'd in, and sacrilegious prince
Did praise his Gods of mettal, wood, and stone,
Protectors of his Crown, and Babylon,
But he above, his doings did deride,
And with a hand soon dashed all this pride.
The King upon the wall casting his eye,
The fingers of a hand writing did spy,
Which horrid sight, he fears must needs portend
Destruction to his Crown, to's Person end.
With quaking knees, and heart appall'd he cries,
For the Soothsayers, and Magicians wise;
This language strange to read, and to unfold;
With gifts of Scarlet robe, and Chain of gold,
And highest dignity, next to the King,
To him that could interpret, clear this thing:
But dumb the gazing Astrologers stand,
Amazed at the writing, and the hand.

None answers the affrighted Kings intent,
Who still expects some fearful sad event;
As dead, alive he sits, as one undone:
In comes the Queen, to chear her heartless Son.
Of Daniel tells, who in his grand-sires dayes
VVas held in more account then now he was.
Daniel in haste is brought before the King,
VVho doth not flatter, nor once cloak the thing;
Reminds him of his Grand-Sires height and fall,
And of his own notorious sins withall:
His Drunkenness, and his profaness high,
His pride and sottish gross Idolatry.
The guilty King with colour pale and dead
Then hears his Mene and his Tekel read.
And one thing did worthy a King (though late)
Perform'd his word to him that told his fate.
That night victorious Cyrus took the town,
VVho soon did terminate his life and crown;
VVith him did end the race of Baladan:
And now the Persian Monarchy began.
The End of the Assyrian Monarchy.

The Romane Monarchy, Being The Fourth And Last, Beginning Anno Mundi , 3213.

Prologue
After some dayes of rest, my restless heart
To finish what's begun, new thoughts impart,
And maugre all resolves, my fancy wrought
This fourth to th'other three, now might be brought:
Shortness of time and inability,
Will force me to a confus'd brevity.
Yet in this Chaos, one shall easily spy
The vast Limbs of a mighty Monarchy,
What e're is found amiss take in good part,
As faults proceeding from my head, not heart.
Stout Romulus, Romes founder, and first King,
Whom vestal Rhea to the world did bring;
His Father was not Mars as some devis'd,
But Æmulus in Armour all disguiz'd:
Thus he deceiv'd his Neece, she might not know
The double injury he then did do.
Where sheperds once had Coats & sheep their folds
Where Swains & rustick Peasants kept their holds,
A City fair did Romulus erect,
The Mistress of the World, in each respect,
His brother Rhemus there by him was slain,

For leaping o're the wall with some disdain.
The stones at first was cemented with blood,
And bloody hath it prov'd, since first it stood.
This City built and Sacrifices done,
A Form of Government, he next begun;
A hundred Senators he likewise chose,
And with the style of Patres, honoured those,
His City to replenish, men he wants,
Great priviledges then to all he grants;
That will within those strong built walls reside,
And this new gentle Government abide.
Of wives there was so great a scarcity,
They to their neighbours sue for a supply;
But all disdain Alliance, then to make,
So Romulus was forc'd this course to take:
Great shews he makes at Tilt and Turnament,
To see these sports, the Sabins all are bent.
Their daughters by the Romans then were caught,
Then to recover them a Field was fought;
But in the end, to final peace they come,
And Sabins as one people dwelt in Rome.
The Romans now more potent 'gin to grow,
And Fedinates they wholly overthrow.
But Romulus then comes unto his end.
Some feigning to the Gods he did ascend:
Others the seven and thirtyeth of his reign,
Affirm, that by the Senate he was slain.
Numa Pompilius.
Numa Pompilius next chose they King,
Held for his piety some sacred thing,
To Janus he that famous Temple built:
Kept shut in peace, set ope when blood was spilt;
Religious Rites and Customes instituted,
And Priests and Flamines likewise he deputed,
Their Augurs strange, their gestures and attire,
And vestal maids to keep the holy fire.
The Nymph Ægeria this to him told,
So to delude the people he was bold:
Forty three years he rul'd with general praise,
Accounted for a God in after dayes.
Tullius Hostilius.
Tullius Hostilius was third Roman King,
Who Martial discipline in use did bring;
War with the antient Albans he did wage,
This strife to end six brothers did ingage.
Three call'd Horatii on the Romans side,
And Curiatii three Albans provide:

The Romans conquer, th'other yield the day,
Yet in their Compact, after false they play.
The Romans sore incens'd, their General slay,
And from old Alba fetch the wealth away;
Of Latin Kings this was long since the Seat,
But now demolished, to make Rome great.
Thirty two years did Tullus reign, then dye,
Left Rome in wealth, and power still growing high.
Ancus Martius.
Next Ancus Martius sits upon the Throne,
Nephew unto Pompilius dead and gone;
Rome he inlarg'd, new built again the wall,
Much stronger, and more beautiful withal;
A stately Bridge he over Tyber made,
Of Boats and Oars no more they need the aid.
Fair Ostia he built this Town, it stood
Close by the mouth of famous Tyber floud,
Twenty four years time of his Royal race,
Then unto death unwillingly gives place.
Tarquinius Priscus
Tarquin a Greek at Corinth born and bred,
Who from his Country for Sedition fled.
Is entertain'd at Rome, and in short time,
By wealth and favour doth to honour climbe;
He after Martius death the Kingdome had,
A hundred Senators he more did add.
Wars with the Latins he again renews,
And Nations twelve of Tuscany subdues,
To such rude triumphs as young Rome then had,
Some State and splendor did this Priscus add:
Thirty eight years (this stronger born) did reign,
And after all, by Ancus Sons was slain.
Servius Tullius.
Next Servius Tullius gets into the Throne,
Ascends not up By merits of his own,
But by the favour and the special grace
Of Tanquil late Queen, obtains the place.
He ranks the people into each degree,
As wealth had made them of ability;
A general Muster takes, which by account,
To eighty thousand Souls then did amount.
Forty four years did Servius Tullius reign,
And then by Tarquin Priscus Son was slain.
Tarquinius Superbus the last King of the Romans
Tarquin the proud, from manners called so,
Sat on the Throne, when he had slain his Foe.
Sextus his Son did most unworthily,

Lucretia force, mirrour of Chastity:
She loathed so the fact, she loath'd her life,
And shed her guiltless blood with guilty knife
Her Husband sore incens'd to quit this wrong,
With Junius Brutus rose, and being strong,
The Tarquins they from Rome by force expel,
In banishment perpetual to dwell;
The Government they change, a new one bring,
And people swear ne'r to accept of King.

www.ingramcontent.com/pod-product-compliance
Lightning Source LLC
Chambersburg PA
CBHW060102050426
42448CB00011B/2590